100 KEYS

FOR YOUR

RIGHT NOW

A SHORT BOOK ON LIFE LESSONS BY

JAVEN

"100 Keys for Your Right Now"

© 2014 by JCM Inc.

Request for permission to quote from this book should be directed to: JCM Inc. PO Box 5767, Hollywood, FL 33083, or contact us by e-mail at info@javenonline.com

Design by Horace Hord

Cover by Eric Ivey

Edited by Suzzette Jules

ISBN: 978-0692206164

Printed in the United States of America

First printing this edition 2014

I dedicate this book to my incredible parents; James and Sylvia Campbell. Although I'm number 12 out of 13, you made me feel like I was number one. I am grateful for your love and leadership.

"100 Keys for Your Right Now"

INTRO:

As the son of a minister and a stay at home mom, life had its share of ups and downs. Nevertheless, the climate in my Hollywood, Florida home was pretty much postcard perfect. Having 12 brothers and sisters gave me the sense that I would never have to face life alone. As a result of loving so many different personalities, I gained the invaluable lesson of empathy and the priceless skill of active listening. Sure, our family had its challenges; but when all is said and done, my experiences and worldview equipped me well for a fruitful career as an entrepreneur, recording artist,   writer, actor, and speaker.

After earning a BA in Psychology and minors in Family Counseling and Biblical Studies, I watched my burgeoning career in the entertainment industry begin to soar. I worked full time for almost 10 years as a minister at a mega-church leading thousands both in leadership and music. With a passion for helping others live more fulfilled lives, I later launched JCM Inc. as a ministry to partner with humanitarian organizations around the globe. As a result, we have toured all over the world to places like Africa, Europe, Brazil, India, China and more doing over 130 dates per year.

In my travels, I realized the need to devote myself even more fully to my faith. My observations, experiences, and the introspective examinations of the life I've developed along the way gave rise to the very book you're holding in your hands. Because it's through faith that one can have and experience great success.

"100 Keys for Your Right Now" is a simple way to open the lines of communication between you and other people and between you and your authentic self. Each of the statements presented here can lead to a deeper discussion and a fuller understanding of your world and the people you meet along the way.

It's my hope that as you read each statement, you will gain greater insight of the beauty of life and the fulfillment of your destiny. Each of these statements carries with it the promise of comprehending the role of purpose and communication as you journey through life and its lessons. My sincere wish is that you feel as uplifted and spiritually nourished reading this book as I did writing it. This book is intended to be a treat that's meant to be shared, discussed, disseminated, and integrated into your daily living. I invite you to begin your journey toward a deeper and more meaningful experience as you turn each page.

For those who don't have the time to read lengthy books, short books are a wonderful way to gain encouragement and knowledge.

Sincerely,

Jáven

Phil 1:6

You should calm down before
speaking your **MIND**

Sometimes what you think at the
moment is not what you mean for
the **FUTURE**

Arrogance as a **YOUTH**
will lead to failure as an adult

"100 Keys for Your Right Now"

The things you refuse to
CONFRONT
will someday **CONQUER** you

In **LIFE** you don't get what you deserve

You get what you can Negotiate

"100 Keys for Your Right Now"

Life has a way of lifting you **UP**
only to let you
DOWN so enjoy the ride

"100 Keys for Your Right Now"

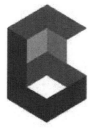

Life is sometimes Wasted on the living

"100 Keys for Your Right Now"

There will always be someone somewhere who will have a problem with you because of **WHO YOU ARE**

"100 Keys for Your Right Now"

MONEY solves most if not **ALL** of Life's Problems

Good Partnerships lead to Good **SUCCESS**

Even the best of **FRIENDS** will sometimes let you **DOWN**

Being **ALONE** can be Fun
Educational
and Sad **ALL**
at the same Time

"100 Keys for Your Right Now"

PEOPLE everywhere think their way is the Right Way

Getting **OLDER** is a real **TRUTH** that demands **RESPECT**

Yesterdays never come **AGAIN**

Remind yourself of **YOUR AGE** so you don't **THINK** like a **CHILD** when it comes to tough **DECISIONS**

The wealthy **DETERMINE** most **THINGS** in Society

It's better to be **HEARD** than to Speak

Speaking **TOO** much can lead to **NO ONE** Listening

A **SMILE** preceding Words can Open Many Doors

YOU cannot Blame yourself for your Children's Choices

They are people too and have a **RIGHT** to their own **DESTINY**

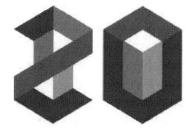

Worship is saying,
"God you see **ME**"

Life is designed to Challenge you

DON'T let the Challenges become your Struggles

"100 Keys for Your Right Now"

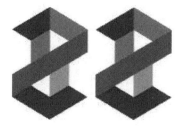

Family, Love, and Friendship
are vital ingredients to
HEALTHY LIVING

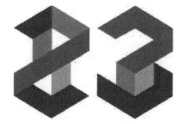

YOU can be alone without being
Lonely when you
LOVE YOURSELF

"100 Keys for Your Right Now"

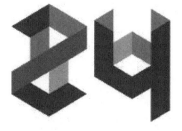

Your **FAMILY** will be virtually the only
REAL PEOPLE
who will see you Through Life until your Death

"100 Keys for Your Right Now"

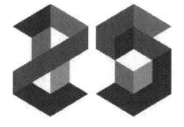

LOVE is the best **FERTILIZER**
for
LIFE

"100 Keys for Your Right Now"

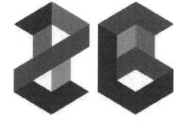

LOVE can never be Captured in **A** Vessel
because it's forever **BIGGER** than you

"100 Keys for Your Right Now"

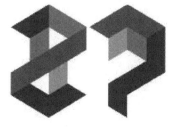

You shouldn't get rid of your
FRIENDS
just because you get Married

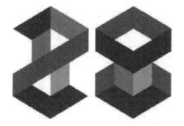

Grow **OLD** with the people who really
Know you and still **LIKE** you

"100 Keys for Your Right Now"

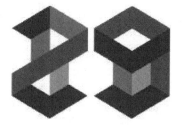

FAMILY loves at all times and at all times
it's important to Love Your Family

"100 Keys for Your Right Now"

A broken **HEART** won't kill you unless you
LET IT

The people that can't **GROW** with you
can't **GO** with you

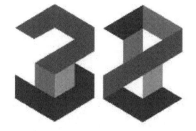

Don't take **TOO** long of a **BREAK**
from Love
because it may take a Break from
YOU

"100 Keys for Your Right Now"

TIME and **SPACE** can help You
Get Over **ANYTHING**

IF you're not ready to **GIVE**,
you're Not Ready to be in a
RELATIONSHIP

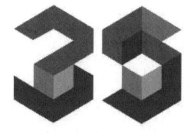

Ask Yourself the Right questions
FIRST
before asking them of the person
you're looking to **DATE**

"100 Keys for Your Right Now"

The more **COMPLETE** you are within Yourself the better you'll be as a mate in your **RELATIONSHIP**

"100 Keys for Your Right Now"

THERE are more Important **THINGS** than love when it comes to a Good Relationship

What's **LOVE** got to do with it? Not as Much as you **THINK**

"100 Keys for Your Right Now"

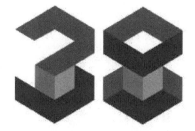

ALWAYS Look People in the **EYE** when discussing a Subject Serious enough to
ALTER your **LIFE**

"100 Keys for Your Right Now"

MOST people have gone Through **A LOT** before meeting you

DON'T add to the **DRAMA**

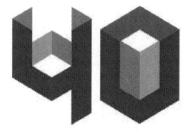

Sometimes a simple **TOUCH** at the right time says it **ALL**

Try to be the **PERSON** who gives
your **LOVED** ones
the Biggest Smile of the **DAY**

"100 Keys for Your Right Now"

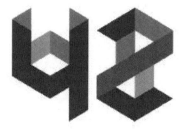

Motivation **GIVES** you Energy
and Energy **MOTIVATES** you

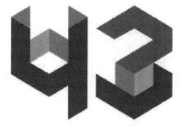

CHANGE comes to those who are
still Living so
EXPECT IT

"100 Keys for Your Right Now"

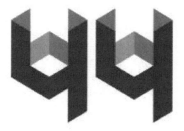

THE most Important thing in Life
is
FAITH

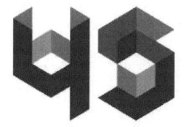

You may Not always do Great but you **CAN** Always do **BETTER**

"100 Keys for Your Right Now"

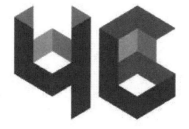

We're all **ONE ADJUSTMENT** away from making our Lives **WORK**

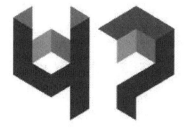

Real **LEADERSHIP** can be
defined as the act of one Beggar
letting the other Beggars
know where the **BREAD** is

"100 Keys for Your Right Now"

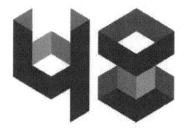

You can't Expect people to **SEE** in you what you don't see in **YOURSELF**

"100 Keys for Your Right Now"

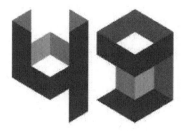

God doesn't call the Qualified
He qualifies Those who are
CALLED

Anytime you think Things are at the
End start Looking for new
BEGINNINGS

"100 Keys for Your Right Now"

Big **SUCCESS** comes by making
SMALL
Changes

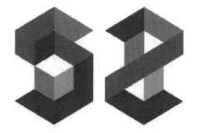

Developing a **PASSION** for
something
Will Lead to great **PURPOSE**

"100 Keys for Your Right Now"

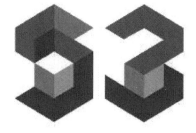

If you **ADMIT** your Failures
you'll **APPRECIATE** your
Accomplishments

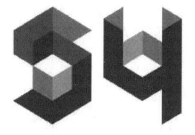

A good **LEADER** is
a good **FOLLOWER**

"100 Keys for Your Right Now"

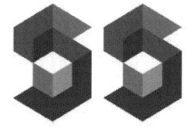

PLEASING people Too Much will rob you of your LIFE

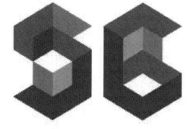

A Winning **ATTITUDE**
can help **YOU**
conquer most problems

"100 Keys for Your Right Now"

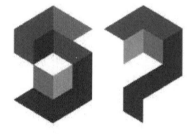

The Loss of a loved one is Life's
Way of
telling
you it is your time to **LEAD**

"100 Keys for Your Right Now"

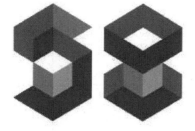

ATTITUDE really does determine
ALTITUDE
You can bring your life Up or
Down just by
Adjusting your Attitude

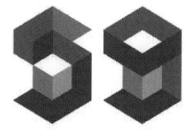

You have been designed to Move
Forward
Everything Positive on your body
FACES forward

"100 Keys for Your Right Now"

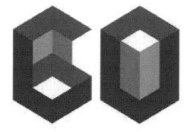

LIFE gets Harder when you Fight
it
and Easier when you **EMBRACE** it

"100 Keys for Your Right Now"

Don't Count how many **TIMES**
you fail

It **IS** a number that Won't Matter
when you **SUCCEED**

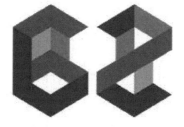

Keep your head **UP** even if that means
Leaning Back
REST can be the best way to
SUCCEED

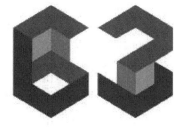

Being **WEALTHY** is not about how Much
Money you have but
about how Many **OPTIONS** you have

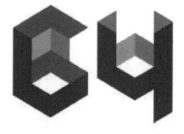

You **DON'T** have what it takes
to fit
everyone else's **PLAN**

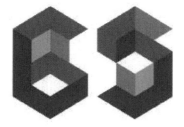

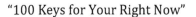

In Life what matters is Who you are
and
what You were meant to **BRING** to
the table

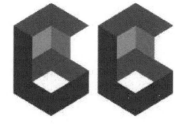

Your Level of Faith will determine
your Level of **GROWTH**

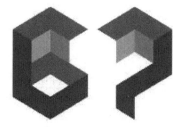

You have to **INVEST** in your
future
If you won't
then Don't **EXPECT** that others
WILL

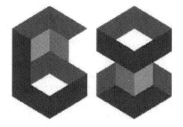

You have to first Love the **IDEA** of
Winning in order to **WIN**

"100 Keys for Your Right Now"

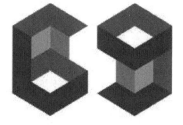

First **BELIEVE** you can make a
Difference in order to make one

Believe you can and You Will

"100 Keys for Your Right Now"

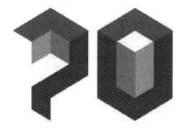

Your **FAITH** can take you Further than your **FEARS**

"100 Keys for Your Right Now"

Anything can become a
DISTRACTION
if you **LET** it

Be **RESPONSIBLE** with your Gift
and
Calling

"100 Keys for Your Right Now"

There **ARE** always new
SOLUTIONS for
a **PROSPEROUS LIFE**

"100 Keys for Your Right Now"

SPENDING is a lot Easier than
Saving

Take the harder way

Children Grow Up and Leave the
nest
so make sure you have something
Else to do
LATER in Life

"100 Keys for Your Right Now"

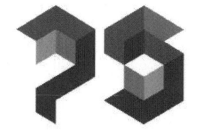

Your **RACE** matters even if you
think it doesn't

KNOW your **CULTURE** even if
you
Never
refer to it in Life

"100 Keys for Your Right Now"

Never forget to forgive and never
forgive to forget

People who are good at making
EXCUSES are
usually No Good at making
Anything else

"100 Keys for Your Right Now"

You can **CHANGE** the outside
World by
changing your Inside World

If you Don't Stick your
FEELINGS out there
they Won't get hurt

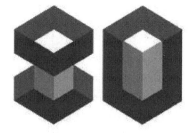

You can't **HELP** someone Who won't **LISTEN**

You don't have to **FEEL** Like
going on
in order to Go On

Just start **MOVING** Forward

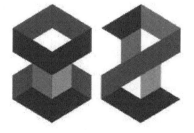

Control can be An **ILLUSION**

"100 Keys for Your Right Now"

Every **SACRIFICE** you make for
Someone **ELSE**
may bring about a Sacrifice
Someone
will make for **YOU**

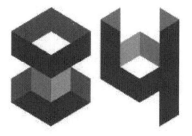

You May not Realize it but **MOST** people don't have it as **GOOD** as You

Always be Helpful when **YOU CAN**

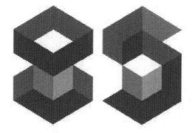

Sometimes **YOU** have to **FIGHT**
even
When **YOU** are **WEAK**

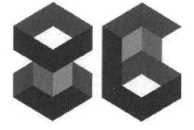

It's important to Keep your **EYES**
Focused on **YOUR** assignment

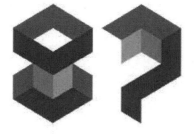

You Don't have to **KNOW**
everything
but
you should be **AWARE** of
everything

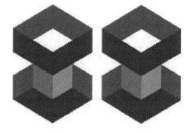

Never Give Away Your
CONFIDENCE

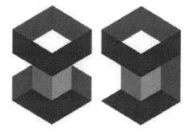

There are battles that are Worth
Fighting even if they may **KILL**
You

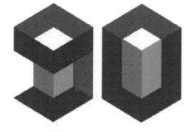

Never Fear death when
Fighting for **VICTORY**

You Can sometimes tell how
SUCCESSFUL you are
by the **SIZE** of the **PROBLEMS**
you're **FACING**

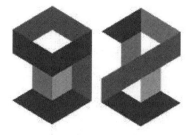

PATIENCE can sometimes be
Your
most Lethal **WEAPON** in **LIFE**

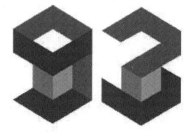

You can Tell how **FAR** your Life
will **GO**
based on The
PEOPLE with whom you Spend
the
Most **TIME**

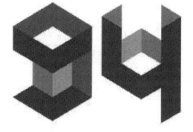

TIME is the most Valuable Thing you Possess

Spend it **WISELY**

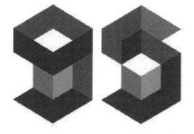

OPPORTUNITIES are not Lost

Someone else just Takes **THEM**

"100 Keys for Your Right Now"

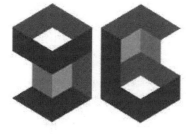

People who don't **RESPECT** your
TIME
don't Respect **YOU**

A Person with no **CONVICTIONS** can be Very Dangerous

"100 Keys for Your Right Now"

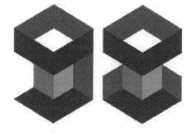

HOW you respond to
CHALLENGES
will determine Your **LEVEL** of
Success

Never **UNDERESTIMATE** the Power of **MUSIC** in your Life

"100 Keys for Your Right Now"

My Dad once Told me that Life is like a **TOLL** Road

You'll either Pay when you get On Or you're **GOING** to **PAY** when you go to **GET OFF**

"100 Keys for Your Right Now"

Visit JAVEN at **www.javenonline.com** to get award-winning music, read motivational articles, and more.

Contact and Booking Information:
JCM/jRock Entertainment
P.O. Box 5767
Hollywood, FL 33083
email: javen@javenmusic.com
phone: 310-467-1840

"100 Keys for Your Right Now"

Follow on Twitter:
www.twitter.com/javenonline

Add JAVEN as a friend on Facebook:
www.facebook.com/TheRealJaven

'Like' the Fan Page:
www.facebook.com/MeetJaven

You Tube

Watch Videos Online:
www.youtube.com/javenonline

Follow JAVEN's travels on Instagram:
www.instagram.com/javenonline

97039270R00113

Made in the USA
Columbia, SC
10 June 2018